SUPERTRUCKS

MEAN MACHINES

130 150

PAUL HARRISON

ARCTURUS

This edition first published in 2012 by Arcturus Publishing

Distributed by Black Rabbit Books
P. O. Box 3263
Mankato
Minnesota MN 56002

Printed in China

Library of Congress Cataloging-in-Publication Data

Harrison, Paul, 1969-
 Supertrucks / by Paul Harrison.
    p. cm. -- (Mean machines)
 Includes index.
 ISBN 978-1-84858-566-9 (hardcover, library bound)
 1. Monster trucks--Juvenile literature. 2. Racing trucks--Juvenile literature. 3. Trucks--Juvenile literature. I. Title.
 TL230.15.H369 2013
 629.224--dc23
                        2011051438

Text: Paul Harrison
Editor: Joe Harris
Design: sprout.uk.com
Cover design: sprout.uk.com

Picture credits:
Cover: Shutterstock: t, bl; Corbis (Transtock): br. Action Plus Sports Images: 20, 21. Austral Int./
Rex Features: 29. Corbis: 3 (Transtock), 5br (Bennett Dean/Eye Ubiquitous), 7 (Neville Elder), 24t,
24b, 25. Ernie Moody/Brooke Dunn/Action Robo,LLC: 8–9, 9tr. Liebherr: 10, 11, 16, 17. Lisatrux: 6.
Martin Uhlmann/pistenbully.com: 18, 19. Oshkoshdefense.com: 14, 15. Rex Features: 30t, 30b, 31.
Rosenbauer: 12, 13. Shutterstock: 1, 4–5, 22, 23, 26–27, 28.

SL002137US

CONTENTS

MACK TITAN ROAD TRAIN

Trucks are the heavyweight champs of the highway. They are bigger and tougher than other vehicles, and are the best way of transporting goods across distances. And trucks don't get any bigger or tougher than the super-long road trains.

Road trains usually pull between two and four trailers. All sorts of goods are carried, from cars to cattle, and from fuel to food.

In 2006 a Mack Titan truck pulled 113 trailers at once—a world record!

Australia is a big country, and its population is scattered over a huge area. It is expensive to transport goods across the country, because of fuel costs over long distances. The solution is road trains. These are really long trucks, which can carry far more than a normal truck.

Road trains have huge, powerful engines, but their power is used for pulling, not for speed.

The top speed of the Titan is a measly 46 mph (75 km/h).

SUPER STATS

MACK TITAN
LENGTH: 26 ft. (7.95 m)
HEIGHT: 13 ft., 9 in. (4.2 m)
WEIGHT: 197 tons (180,000 kg)
ENGINE: 605 bhp
TOP SPEED: 46 mph (75 km/h)

MEAN MACHINES

BIGFOOT MONSTER TRUCK

Monster trucks are like pickup trucks, but with a big twist. They have huge wheels and massive tires—more than big enough to drive right over anything that gets in their way. People come from far and wide to see them.

Bigfoot 17 is the only version of Bigfoot based in Europe full-time.

Bigfoot 17 can travel at 80 mph (129 km/h) and can jump a line of cars from a ramp.

The people who build the Bigfoot trucks must be superstitious. There has never been a Bigfoot 13.

Monster trucks perform in special shows.
They race against each other or crush cars under their massive wheels. Several famous monster trucks have been called Bigfoot. There have actually been 18 versions of Bigfoot—and they have won 29 championships between them.

Bigfoot 5 has the biggest wheels of any monster truck. The tires alone are 9.8 ft. (3 m) tall. It's also the widest truck around.

Bigfoot 5 weighs around 14 tons (12,700 kg), making it the heaviest monster truck in the world.

Bigfoot 5 is on permanent display outside a garage in St. Louis.

SUPER STATS

BIGFOOT 17
LENGTH: 18 ft. (5.5 m)
HEIGHT: 10 ft. (3 m)
WEIGHT: 4.7 tons (4,300 kg)
WHEELS: 4
ENGINE: 1750 bhp (estimated)
TOP SPEED: 80 mph (129 km/h)

ROBOSAURUS

The biggest and best monster trucks are stars in their own right. They try to outdo each other to be the most outrageous. Some can transform into weird-looking creatures. The car-eating Robosaurus is a monster truck in every sense!

The jaws have 89,000 Newtons (20,000 lbs.) of biting force. That's 30 times more powerful than a lion's bite.

The driver sits inside Robosaurus's head.

The pincers are moved by a hydraulic system. Hydraulic systems use liquids to help move heavy weights.

Each of the front wheels can move independently. This makes it easier to move Robosaurus around.

Robosaurus is a 40-foot (12-m) high stunt truck. It can crush cars in its vicelike grip, or chew them to pieces in its powerful jaws. It can even breathe fire, as if it were a metal-plated dragon. Like any other truck, Robosaurus has wheels for moving around. However, it is not going to win any races!

Robosaurus can fold up like a real-life Transformer and turn into a trailer unit. It can then be attached to another truck and can be towed from place to place.

SUPER STATS

ROBOSAURUS

LENGTH: (in trailer mode) 46 ft., 9 in. (14.26 m)

HEIGHT: 40 ft. (12.2 m)

WEIGHT: 29 tons (26,300 kg)

WHEELS: 12

ENGINE: 500 bhp

TOP SPEED: Unknown—but very slow!

MEAN MACHINES

LIEBHERR T 282 C

You need a truly massive truck to take on the toughest jobs—jobs such as working in a quarry. Quarrying is a type of mining where the top layer of the ground is dug away. Giant machines are used for digging itself, and equally huge vehicles are needed to move all the rubble away.

The 282 C can carry a load of up 400 tons (363 tonnes).

The driver needs cameras and monitors to help him see what is around the truck.

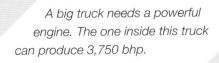

A big truck needs a powerful engine. The one inside this truck can produce 3,750 bhp.

The 282 C stands more than 26 feet (8 m) high and is more than 31 feet (9.5 m) wide.

The Liebherr T 282 C is no ordinary dump truck. This mammoth machine's job is to carry away the rocks, gravel, and soil dug up by excavators. The bigger the dump truck, the more soil it can carry. As the biggest dump truck around, the T 282 C can carry 30 times more soil than normal dumpers.

The truck might be big, but it isn't fast. It has a top speed of only 40 mph (65 km/h).

Powerful hydraulics tip the back of the truck upward to empty it.

SUPER STATS

LIEBHERR T 282 C
LENGTH: 51 ft., 6 in. (15.69 m)
HEIGHT: 27 ft., 3 in. (8.29 m)
WEIGHT: 261 tons (237,000 kg)
WHEELS: 6
ENGINE: 3750 bhp
TOP SPEED: 40 mph (65 km/h)

ROSENBAUER
PANTHER

The most awesome supertrucks don't just transport goods—they save lives. Giant rescue vehicles such as the Rosenbauer Panther firetruck come with all sorts of special equipment. The Panther has floodlights, hoses, huge water tanks, and an extending turret!

Speed is of the essence when tackling fires. The cab is designed so that the six crew members can get out in less than ten seconds.

A powerful 665 bhp engine can push the Panther to speeds of 75 mph (120 km/h)— which is fast for a big, heavy truck.

Nozzles beneath the truck can put out fires that are on the ground.

Big wheels help the Panther to travel over grass or rough terrain if necessary.

Hard-to-reach fires can be tackled by an extending turret. This can reach up to 52 ft. (16 m) high.

The Rosenbauer Panther is very different from the average firetruck. The Panther has been designed especially for airports. It is perfectly adapted for speeding down runways and for tackling the sorts of fire that might break out on an aircraft.

The Panther has large tanks for carrying foam and water.

Hoses are rewound electronically once the fire is out.

SUPER STATS

ROSENBAUER PANTHER 6X6
LENGTH: 38 ft., 9 in. (11.8 m)
HEIGHT: 11 ft., 10 in. (3.6 m)
WEIGHT: 34 tons (31,000 kg)
WHEELS: 6
ENGINE: 665 bhp
TOP SPEED: 75 mph (120 km/h)

OSHKOSH PLS

Trucks transport goods all over the globe, using road networks. But what happens when roads have been badly damaged, or no roads exist? Well, then you need a truck that can tackle tough terrain—a truck that dares to go places others wouldn't dream of. You need the Oshkosh PLS.

The PLS is used to carry everything from ammunition to food.

Big wheels are ideal for traveling over rough ground.

The PLS (Palletised Load System) can also tow a specially designed trailer unit. This trailer can also hold loads of up to 18.5 tons (16,000 kg) in weight.

The Oshkosh PLS is used by the armed forces. This often means that it has to deal with some really hostile environments. The terrain might be rough, so the PLS has to be good at traveling off-road. Plus the truck might be working in a war zone, so it has to be built to keep its driver as safe as possible.

The PLS has a special arm at the back. This is used for dragging containers on board. This can be done without the driver's leaving the cab.

Armor-plating can be added to the cab unit.

The engine sends power to all ten wheels. This helps to keep the PLS moving when traveling off-road.

SUPER STATS

OSHKOSH PLS
LENGTH: 36 ft. (11 m)
HEIGHT: 10 ft., 9 in. (3.28 m)
WEIGHT: 27,5 tons (24,800 kg)
WHEELS: 10
ENGINE: 500 bhp
TOP SPEED: 57 mph (92 km/h)

LIEBHERR LTM 11200-9.1 MOBILE CRANE

When it comes to lifting and moving heavy objects, there's no better machine than a crane. However, cranes take a long time to put up, and just as long to take down. What's the solution if you're in a hurry? A mobile crane, like the LTM 11200-9.1, could be the answer.

Cranes would topple over unless they had a weight called a "counterweight" to balance them. This crane's counterweight weighs 222.5 tons (202 tonnes).

The amount of weight the crane can carry depends on how far it has to reach out. The farther it has to reach, the lighter the load has to be.

The boom (the crane's arm) is telescopic, which means its parts can slide into each other.

The Liebherr LTM 11200-9.1 has the longest telescopic boom in the world. It can stretch up to 330 feet (101 m) into the air! As a mobile crane, the LTM 11200-9.1 can be set up very quickly. It can also work in a much smaller space than a normal crane.

The rear wheels can be steered too, to help move the crane around tight spots.

This crane lifts loads of up to 1,325 tons (1,200 tonnes).

SUPER STATS

LIEBHERR LTM 11200-9.1
LENGTH: 65 ft., 5 in. (19.94 m)
HEIGHT: 13 ft. (4 m)
WEIGHT: 106 tons (96,000 kg)
WHEELS: 18
ENGINE: 680 bhp
TOP SPEED: 47 mph (75 km/h)

PISTENBULLY 600 W

The wheel may be one of the greatest inventions in history, but wheels are useless in snow. Trucks called snowcats have a clever way of dealing with this: caterpillar tracks. The PistenBully 600 W is a snowcat used for maintaining ski slopes. It can tackle deep snow and steep hills.

The tracks are made from steel or steel and rubber combined.

This winch attachment makes it easier to push large amounts of snow uphill.

Snowcats can have either two sets of tracks or four. Four-track snowcats are more maneuvrable.

MEAN MACHINES

The problem with wheels and snow is surface area. The weight of a truck is carried by the parts of the tires touching the ground. This is too much weight on too small an area for a soft surface like snow. The result is that the truck sinks.

Work on ski slopes is often done at night when the skiers have gone. Powerful lights make working in the dark much easier.

The PistenBully 600 W comes with a snowplow attachment at the front and a winch at the back.

SUPER STATS

PISTENBULLY 600 W
LENGTH: 30 ft. (9.13 m)
HEIGHT: (without winch) 9 ft., 5 in. (2.88 m)
WEIGHT: (with steel tracks) 12.5 tons (11,215 kg)
WHEELS: two caterpillar tracks
ENGINE: 400 bhp
TOP SPEED: 12 mph (20 km/h)

MAN RACING TRUCK

Drivers often complain about getting stuck behind slow-moving trucks on busy roads. However, not all trucks move like snails. Some trucks are even built for racing! They compete on racing circuits in front of cheering crowds. It takes a real supertruck to do well in this battle of the titans.

MAN trucks have won the European Truck Racing Championships 11 times.

Normal road-going trucks have their engines right at the front. Race trucks move the engines farther back to keep the truck balanced.

Racing rules insist that trucks have their speed limited to 100 mph (161 km/h).

Truck racing used to be between normal road-going trucks. Slowly the sport has developed and now truck manufacturers compete against each other. Racing is good publicity for truck makers—especially if their trucks are winning. One of the most successful manufacturers is the German truck maker MAN.

The trucks don't race with the trailer attached!

Special strengthening bars, called a roll cage, must be fitted to the cab in case of the truck tipping over.

Many engines have turbochargers. These push more air into the engine, which increases the engine's power.

Race trucks' engines are twice as powerful as normal road trucks' engines.

SUPER STATS

MAN RACING TRUCK
LENGTH: (estimated) 20 ft., 4 in. (6.2 m)
HEIGHT: (estimated) 9 ft., 8 in. (3 m)
WEIGHT: 6 tons (5,500 kg)
WHEELS: 6
ENGINE: 1,000 bhp
TOP SPEED: 100 mph (161 km/h)

Jostling for position between trucks often leads to bashing and crashing, although this is officially discouraged.

SHOCKWAVE

Racing trucks may be fast, but they are not the fastest trucks around—not by a long way. For a really fast truck, you need to check out Shockwave. This jet-powered speed machine was originally a normal truck made by a company called Peterbilt. It's had a lot of changes!

The type of jet engines that power Shockwave have also been used in planes used to train jet pilots.

Shockwave won its world record by traveling at an unbelievable 376 mph (605 km/h)— that's faster than a Formula 1 racing car!

Shockwave travels so fast that it needs two parachutes to help slow it down.

Shockwave holds the record for being the world's fastest truck. It can achieve truly blistering speeds thanks to its super-powerful jet engines. Jet engines squash air and fuel together to generate enormous power. And just for good measure, Shockwave has three of them!

By burning diesel fuel, Shockwave can make an impressive fire display!

The engines are tilted upward at a slight angle to help keep Shockwave from lifting off the ground.

Shockwave is a popular attraction at monster truck shows and air shows.

SUPER STATS

SHOCKWAVE
LENGTH: 21 ft., 8 in. (6.6 m)
HEIGHT: Not known
WEIGHT: 3.5 tons (3,175 kg)
WHEELS: 6
ENGINE: 36,000 bhp
TOP SPEED: 376 mph (605 km/h)

MEAN MACHINES

HUMVEE

Tough situations call for tough trucks. Soldiers often find themselves in seriously dangerous places. They need trucks that are as at home driving off-road as they are rolling down the highway. Fortunately for the army, there's a truck that meets their needs. It's called the Humvee.

The Humvee can drive through water more than 5 ft. (1.5 m) deep.

The engine sends power to all four wheels—this is called four-wheel drive.

Big chunky tires provide lots of grip on slippery or loose surfaces. Slopes of up to 60% are no problem for the Humvee.

The real name for the Humvee is the HMMWV. That stands for "High Mobility Multipurpose Wheeled Vehicle." The Humvee's reputation for being rugged and reliable meant people who weren't in the army wanted to own one too. As a result, a civilian version was made. It is called the Hummer.

The first person to own a Hummer was actor Arnold Schwarzenegger. It was his idea to ask the Humvee manufacturers to make a civilian version.

Hummers were liked and loathed in equal measure. People loved their off-road ability, but hated their width and the amount of fuel they used.

Production of the Hummers stopped in 2010.

SUPER STATS

HMMWV M1165A1
LENGTH: 16 ft., 2 in. (4.93 m)
HEIGHT: 6 ft., 3 in. (1.91 m)
WEIGHT: 3.6 tons (3,338 kg)
WHEELS: 4
ENGINE: 3,400 bhp
TOP SPEED: 70 mph (113 km/h)

ARMORED TRUCKS

Some kinds of cargo need heavy-duty protection. When armies transport soldiers, or banks transport money, they move these valuable assets in armored vehicles. The Patria PASI is a six-wheeled, armored troop transporter or ambulance.

As a troop transporter, the Patria PASI can carry seven people.

The long pole at the front is actually a flagpole.

Depending on how the Patria is set up it can weigh as much as 25.5 tons (23,000 kg).

SVESKEN

The heavy armor plating weighs down the Patria, so it's not fast. Its top speed is only 60 mph (96 km/h).

MEAN MACHINES

An armored truck is, in effect, a mobile fort. It is designed to resist even the most determined attackers. The army uses armored vehicles such as Patria PASI, which can do several different jobs. In civilian life, armored trucks can sometimes be seen carrying money or valuables from shops to banks.

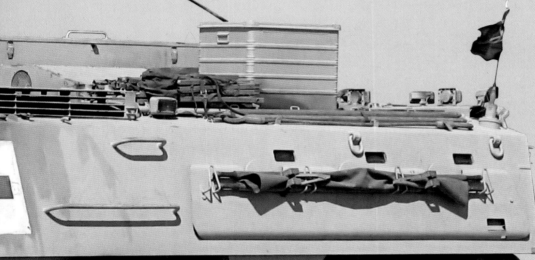

The truck's casing and its windows are bulletproof.

The truck can still drive even if the tires are punctured.

The underneath of the Patria is especially strengthened to protect it against mines.

SUPER STATS

PATRIA PASI
LENGTH: 27 ft., 9 in. (8.47 m)
HEIGHT: (with tower) 11 ft., 4 in. (3.45 m)
WEIGHT: 25.5 tons (23,000 kg)
WHEELS: 6
ENGINE: 270 bhp
TOP SPEED: 60 mph (96 km/h)

CUSTOMIZED TRUCKS

There are many amazing trucks in the world, but very few are unique. If you want something that really is one of kind, you will have to do it yourself! This is called customizing. In places such as Japan and Pakistan, they have taken customization to a whole new level.

Despite all the changes, most dekotora are still allowed to drive on the road.

Decorations include neon lights, paintings, and adding lots of pipes.

Japanese customized trucks are called "dekotora." This means decorated trucks. They look very high-tech and futuristic. Owners meet up at dekotora shows, which draw large crowds of spectators.

In Pakistan, old trucks are often customized by street artists. They are decorated with different materials as well as paintings. Wood, metal, plastic, and reflective strips can be seen.

The trucks are covered in religious paintings, humorous sayings, and pictures of the "evil eye."

Trucks from different regions of Pakistan use different materials in their decorations.

The customized trucks of Pakistan can take up to five weeks to decorate.

SUPER STATS

These symbols and materials are typical of different regions of Pakistan.

DECORATION	REGION
Peacocks	Punjab
Carved wooden doors	Swat
Camel bone	Sindh
Plastic	Rawalpindi
Reflective tape	Karachi

FUTURE TRUCKS

Truck manufacturers are always thinking about the future. How can they make their vehicles faster, smarter, and greener? They try out their ideas with concept trucks. One of the most amazing looking designs is called the Chameleon. Its body can change size depending on what it is transporting.

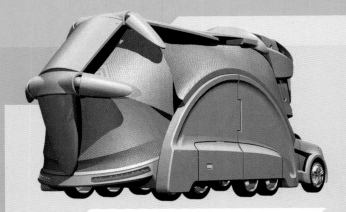

The designer was inspired by the way a centipede's body is made up of different segments.

Lots of glass gives the driver a good all-round view.

Future trucks will be as aerodynamic as possible. The more easily they move through the air, the less fuel they will use.

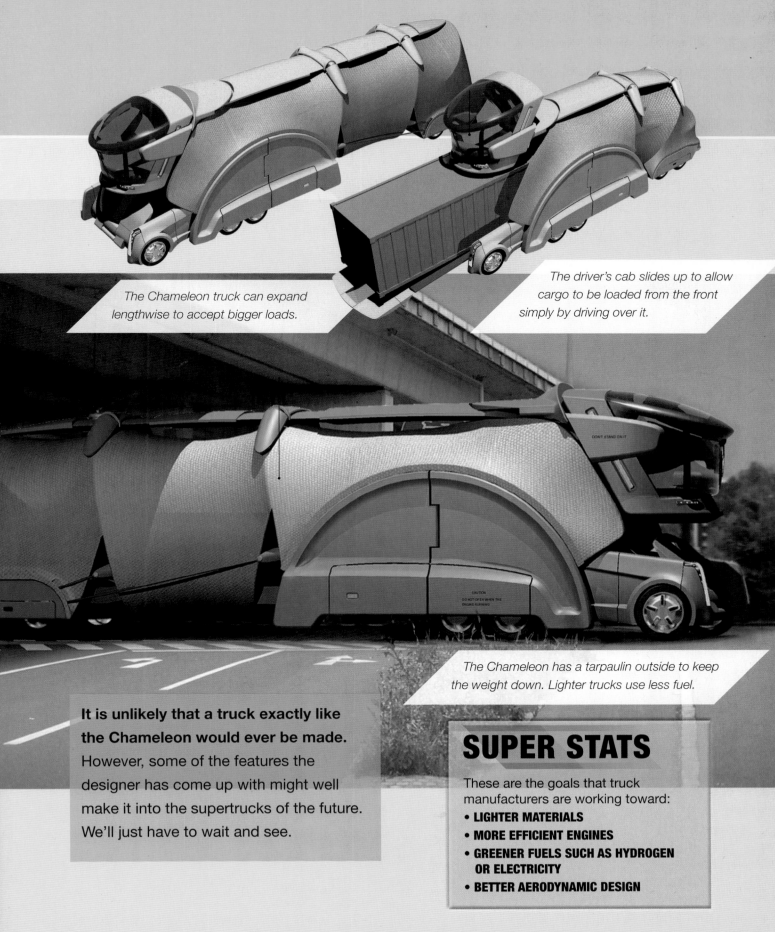

The Chameleon truck can expand lengthwise to accept bigger loads.

The driver's cab slides up to allow cargo to be loaded from the front simply by driving over it.

The Chameleon has a tarpaulin outside to keep the weight down. Lighter trucks use less fuel.

It is unlikely that a truck exactly like the Chameleon would ever be made. However, some of the features the designer has come up with might well make it into the supertrucks of the future. We'll just have to wait and see.

SUPER STATS

These are the goals that truck manufacturers are working toward:

- **LIGHTER MATERIALS**
- **MORE EFFICIENT ENGINES**
- **GREENER FUELS SUCH AS HYDROGEN OR ELECTRICITY**
- **BETTER AERODYNAMIC DESIGN**

GLOSSARY

bhp a measurement of the power of an engine. This stands for "brake horsepower."

boom a long arm, as on a crane

caterpillar tracks wheels with a steel band around the outside, which helps them to travel across difficult terrain

chrome a highly reflective metal covering

counterweight a weight that is used to stop something falling over

customize to make changes to something, so that it fits your individual needs

excavator a digging machine

hostile unfriendly or dangerous

hydraulic powered by a liquid forced through tubes under pressure

population the people who live in a particular area

terrain the shape of an area of land, and the features of that area, such as trees

vice a tool with movable jaws that can be used to hold something still

winch a machine for pulling objects up

FURTHER READING

Daynes, Katie. *Usborne Beginners: Trucks.* Usborne, 2007.

DK Publishing. *Monster Jam: The Amazing Guide.* DK Children, 2001.

Oxlade, Chris. *Trucks Inside and Out.* PowerKids Press, 2009.

Young, Jeff C. *Trucks: The Ins and Outs of Monster Trucks, Semis, Pickups, and Other Trucks.* Capstone Press, 2010.

INDEX